How to turn Garbage into Gold: 101 Items You can find at Thrift stores and Garage Sales to sell on Ebay.

Introduction

I want to thank you and congratulate you for downloading the book, *"How to turn Garbage into Gold:101 Things You can find at Thrift Stores and Garage Sales to sell on Ebay"*.

This book contains multiple items you may be able to find just about anywhere "junk" is sold. The mantra here is to buy these items inexpensively and sell them for what they are actually worth online which in turn makes you profit.

This book is not legal advice. It's more of a guide to point you in the right direction of items to look for when you enter a thrift store or a flea market.

I like to think I'm a nerd and a hipster so there's a lot of things in this book that are based towards those niches. I know the items in those categories and in the art of flipping items you can't have too much knowledge.

Please keep in mind that any values in this guide are as of late 2014. Please research out the current value before purchasing. I can't guarantee these items will stay the same value forever!

KNOWLEDGE IS POWER. While the other guys are trying to research the value of something in the lock case using the Ebay app on their smartphones I'm able to take the Pokemon Gameboy Color games straight to the cash register because I know that they will sell every single time.

You're about to read about 101 great items. Study it and get going!

And whatever you do... Stay out of my Goodwill...

I'm looking at you Tony... WOOF WOOF, YO.

1 - Chip 'n Dale Rescue Rangers

2 - Jurassic Park

3 - Lord of the Rings

4 - Pendleton clothing

5 - Plush toys

6 - Sealed "Deadtech"

7 - Character themed bedsheets

8 - Vintage VHS tapes

9 - Big Mouth Billy Bass

10 - Out of print Audio CDs

11 - Replacement filters

12 – Mugs

13 - Vinyl Records

14 - Needlepoint kits

15 - Puzzles

16 - Harry Potter themed items

17 - Pokemon themed items

18 - Raybans

19 - Classic Picture Books

20 - Handheld electronic games

21 - Converse shoes

22 - Exercise tapes

23 - Tom's Shoes

24 - Serendipity children's books

25 - Hawaiian shirts

26 - Super Nintendo system and games

27 - Disney Reader books

28 - Beanie Boos

29 - The Croods

30 - Comic Books

31 - Scene It board games

32 - Lego sets

33 - Graphic novels

34 - Anime DVD sets

35 - Board games

36 - Sony Walkmen

37 - 1980's nylon jackets

38 - Nike Air Jordans

39 - Pearl snap shirts

40 - Text Books

41 - PC games

42 - Educational PC programs

43 - Dungeons and Dragons

44 - Elf Quest

45 - License plates

46 - Original Star Wars

47 - Transformers

48 - He-Man

49 - Back to the Future

50 - Funko collectibles

51 - Comic Con Exclusives

52 - Casio calculator watches

53 - Seiko watches

54 - Coleman camping gear

55 - Under Armour clothing

56 - Black Dog apparel

57 - Audio books

58 - Language training courses

59 - Stand up Comedy CDs

60 - WWF Wrestling Teddy Bears

61 - Duffy teddy bears

62 - Cook books

63 - Vintage concert shirts

64 - Kickstarter exclusives

65 - Vintage camouflage clothing

66 - External frame backpacks

67 - Vintage sport shirts

68 - Study Bibles

69 - Mystery Science Theater 3000 DVD sets

70 - Magazine back issues

71 - American Girl dolls

72 - Speak 'n Spell sets

73 - Teddy Ruxpin

74 - E.T. the Extra Terrestrial

75 - Vintage airline travel posters

76 - Metal brand signs.

77 - Soft drink themed products

78 - Talkboy

79 - Charlie Brown themed items

80 - Patagonia

81 - Vintage typewriters

82 - Lunchboxes

83 - Kitchen utility replacement parts

84 - Jewelry

85 - Cameras

86 - "Mad Men" themed items

87 - Old Photos

88 - Old Postcards

89 - Harley Davidson themed items

90 - Cast Iron Skillets

91 - Vintage vacuum refill bags

92 - Satin jackets

93 - Bronze material items

94 - "How to play" instrument books

95 - Snapback hats.

96 - Vintage patches

1 - Chip 'n Dale Rescue Rangers

I loved this show growing up in the early 1990s. It was a delight. I realized much later the fact that Chip and Dale are modeled after Indiana Jones and Magnum, P.I.. Hilarious.

This was a great Nintendo game that my sister and I loved playing over and over again. There's nothing like being hit in the head with a tomato while a hulking robot dog tries to eat your face.

Look out for:

the Chip 'n Dale Rescue Rangers 2 NES game

You should be able to buy a NES game for only $5 at a thrift store and this is one you will definitely want to. You'll want to because it's very rare and the cartridge alone will sell for $100. If you can find a complete in box game then it can go for $300 or higher on Ebay.

2 - Jurassic Park

Dinosaurs are on the loose and profits aren't that far behind. I was absolutely in love with this story. My room had a poster with a glow in the dark T. Rex head from the movie on it. I would spend a good 30 minutes every day "charging up" the dinosaur's eye with a flashlight so that I could look up at night and see the glowing eye of the coolest dinosaur that time forgot.

Look out for:

Jurassic Park: Operation Genesis game.

It's an original XBOX game and it's worth a lot of money. I've found this at yard sales and thrift stores for only a few dollars. This will regularly go on Ebay for $70 to $80 dollars.

Bonus:

Jurassic Park "Carnotaurus"action figure

Memorize what this guy looks like because just the figure by itself can go up to $200 dollars plus on Ebay.

This is a classic story that will always be popular in every generation. Keep an eye out for the extended dvd sets and some of the older video games as well.

Look out for:

Vintage Lord of the Rings puzzles from the early 1980s.

The artist "Roger Garland" as illustrator is key here. I have seen this Gandalf themed puzzle pictured above go as high as $250 dollars on Ebay while just the empty puzzle box can go for $100 dollars.

Here's where the hipster comes in. Pendleton shirts are awesome. It's that classic plaid from the 1950s and the blue tag that sells it. Anytime I find one of these shirts it's very hard to part with it but the payout makes it worth it.

Look out for:

The legendary "Dude" sweater from "The Big Lebowski".

Jeff Bridges made this sweater famous when wearing it as "The Dude". If you ever find one of these vintage Pendleton heavy sweaters then you have a great potential profit on your hands. They regularly will go for $350 to $500 on Ebay due to "Lebowski fests" that are held all over the country.

5 - Plush toys

At thrift stores you can always find a great selection of plush toys. Usually they are priced for under a dollar. I always have great success with older plush toys. Just remember to do the sniff test and look for dirt or stains.

What to look for:

Keep an eye out for the "Kohl's Cares" plush toys that come with books sets.

Usually you can find the Dr. Seuss themed ones at thrift stores all over the place. Kids love them and you'll be sure to sell them quickly.

For example:

I found 2 "Pink Fish" plushes that I was able to purchase for $.79 each and then sold for $35 each on Amazon.

6 - Sealed "Deadtech"

"Deadtech" items are new electronics that have never been opened and that are not available for purchase in a "big box" store such as Walmart anymore. You'll be surprised at the never opened electronic devices you'll start to see at thrift stores if you're able to check the same stores a few times weekly.

Deadtech covers a variety of different items, ranging from floppy disks to computer audio cards. Don't be afraid to scan the listings as you may be surprised as to what something is actually worth.

What to look for:

I look for sealed 10 packs of 3.5 inch floppy disks. You can usually buy them for a few dollars and easily get $30 to $40 dollars for them on Amazon or Ebay.

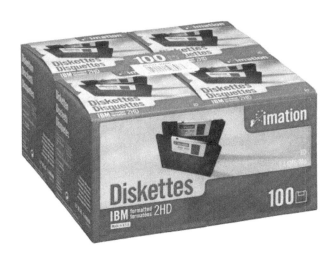

7 - Character themed bedsheets

I know this sounds weird but trust me when I say that crafters and hipsters love this stuff. I'm talking about old bedsheets with characters from the '80s and '90s.

People will pay out the nose on Ebay for the chance to get the special fabric so they can complete their project.

Make sure you carefully inspect the entire bedsheet for stains, tears, etc.

What to look for:

Disney, Peanuts, Star Wars, and Star Trek are all different character brands you should be looking for at

yard sales or thrift stores.

Spend a few dollars and watch it turn into $70 to $80 easy on Ebay.

8 - Vintage VHS tapes

VHS is where it's at. There are some many amazing films that never made the transfer over to DVD that it almost makes me want to get a VCR and a TV to play them with.

If you can find a thrift store that still has VHS tapes in stock then you have found a potential gold mine that will keep refilling itself every week.

I tend to stick with sealed VHS tapes. If they are opened make sure you check to see if the actual advertised tape is in the box.

What to look for:

I could write a whole book about VHS tapes and trust me, I will eventually. Until then, here's one to look for.

WWF Best of RAW Volume 1

This was probably found in a flea market for under a dollar and was sold on Ebay for $350. Wrestling fans will pay for hard to find media items which is a fact you'll want to keep in mind.

9 - Big Mouth Billy Bass

If only I could travel back in time to when this fish lined the walls of every Walmart in the land. I would be, to say it technically, an absolute bazillionaire.

I don't know what it is but people still love this Bass for the walls. It could be because "redneck is in" due to the popularity of the show "Duck Dynasty."

Billy sells every time.

What to look for:

Look for Billy unopened and in the original box at your local flea markets.

I usually buy him for no more than $5 and get $80 to $90 on Ebay or Amazon. Around the holidays I have seen this golden grouper go for up to $150.00 all Christmas long.

10 - Out of print Audio CDs

Most people will say that there is not a market for audio CDs anymore but you can't forget that there are somethings you just can't find on the internet.

Also, if you can find them sealed and put them on the right marketplace the right collector will snatch it up quicker than you can blink.

Know your prices before you list. You don't want to be the one to be hustled, right?

What to look for:

The Ghostbusters sealed soundtrack CD.

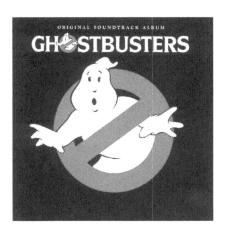

Not only is it the 30th anniversary but it's also an out of print soundtrack as well.

Right now it's selling on Ebay for $100 and if you're lucky you could probably find it at a thrift store for $2 to $3.

11 - Replacement filters

Think out of the box on this one but make sure it's in the box. As in it's never been used. Am I right?

Appliances usually need a filter of some sort. Keep your eyes open for unopened filters at the thrift stores as they can get big money on Ebay. Make sure you check that it is unopened and that there's no past expiration dates if applicable.

What to look for:

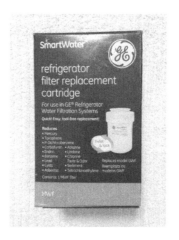

GE Smart Water Refrigerator Filters.

You can find these for a few dollars which in turn will usually sell for $40 to $50 apiece on EBay. The bidding wars will be fierce!

People love their coffee and they love it in a cool mug. There are some serious collectors out there. You need to familiarize yourself with what sells and how to scoop it up quick in the thrift store. Also, learn to how ship a mug without it breaking in transit. Your customer will love you for it.

What to look for:

The 2009 City Collector Series from Starbucks.

Don't laugh. Look for these mugs. They can be worth a lot of money. For example, this Cleveland mug that you could probably get for less than a dollar is selling on Ebay for $200 to $300. Starbucks collectors love their mugs and will pay hundreds of dollars for them.

13 - Vinyl Records

Hipsters love their vinyl records and so should you. This is a category I need to get more into as I know the money is there waiting to be made at every thrift store in the vinyl section.

What to look for:

Here's one example of a valuable vinyl record.

The broken up group "Death Grips" album "Exmilitary" is going for $500 to $600 on Ebay. You could pick it up at a Goodwill for less than $3. It's all about being in the right place at the right time.

14 - Needlepoint kits

Stop judging me. Stop it. There is money in the weirdest things. Always remember that.

You'll want to always look to see that the entire contents of the kit is still in the packaging and that the kit hasn't already been completed.

Great brands to look out for are Dimensions Gold Collection, Bucilla, and Ehrman.

What to look for:

Here's a vintage Looney Tunes "Taz" latch hook kit

I picked this up at a thrift store for $3 and sold it for $75 on Amazon.

15 - Puzzles

Open your eyes and you will find puzzles everywhere in your local thrift store. People still love the unbeatable tactile fun of putting together a puzzle with their hands.

Look for the sealed ones as they can go for a good amount on Ebay. As long as there are nursing homes there will probably be a market for this.

What to look for:

Ravensburger is the brand of puzzles you need to be looking for.

For example, this Neuschwanstein Castle puzzle from Ravensburger sealed and sitting on a Goodwill toy shelf somewhere out there for $5 or less.

Ebay sold listings show this guy going for $500 to $600 regularly. Make sure buyer pays for shipping for this 12,000 piece monster!

16 - Harry Potter themed items

This is a brand that will never go away. It's a story that is now a classic and future generations will continue to discover it for years to come.

What to look for:

If you can find any of the original games from the 2001 time period they seem to do well.

For example:

This 2001 Hogwarts School play set I could see sitting on a flea market shelf for $10 while on Ebay it's selling for around $150.

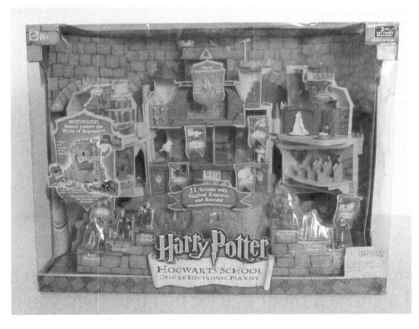

10 points for Gryffindor, indeed.

17 - Pokemon themed items

My generation grew up with the first cycle of Pokemon and now we're trying to buy back those memories we had growing up.

The market for Pokemon is fierce right now.

Look for the original plushes, game boy games, etc. You can find these at about every tag sale.

What to look for:

Keep an eye out for the Pikachu yellow Pokemon game for Game Boy. I've found this for less than a dollar at the local thrift.

It will normally go for $20 to $30 dollars. If you can find all 6 and sell them as a lot together then you can normally sell them for $150 to $180.

18 - Raybans

The Hipster calling card. I'm wearing them right now..

People absolutely love the Rayban brand and you should pick them up every time. I always have my eye out for them and they are hard to find. They're on my bucket list of things to find someday in a thrift store.

What to look for:

The more vintage the pair of glasses is the better chance of large returns for you. That is unless you end up keeping them for yourself. First rule of picker school is NEVER FALL IN LOVE WITH THE MERCHANDISE.

You can pick up glasses for less than $3 at the local garage sale. This pair sold for just under a $1,000. Wow.

19 - Classic Picture Books

These are the books you grew up reading in elementary school. These stories will be used by every teacher for every future generation to come.

Dr. Seuss, Shel Silverstein, and Eric Carle, the authors go on and on. Look through the kids section at your local library to familiarize yourself.

What to look for:

Keep an eye out for older picturebooks such as "A Day in Fairy Land".

I've picked up books like this for less than $3 at the local thrift which can easily go for $40 to $50 on Ebay regularly.

20 - Handheld electronic games

I've noticed a trend around the mall and in the airport. People want to play a game but not be bothered with their cellphone at the same time.

The old handheld electronic games are definitely making a comeback.

What to look for:

Radica and Excalibur are some great brands to keep in mind.

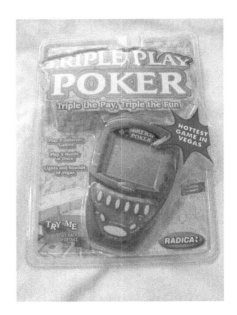

I've found Radica sealed games for up to $5 at the thrift store and some of them, such as this one, can go for up to $90 regularly on Ebay.

21 - Converse shoes

Hipsters love their Chucks. That what Converses are normally called by the community. I found a red pair of high tops at a Goodwill for $3 and had to hold on it. They were my size so don't give me any of that "Don't fall in love with the merchandise" stuff.

What to look for:

Memorize the name "Jack Purcell". If the shoes look really old and have his name on the back then pick them up immediately!

Shoes such as the one pictured will bring $700 to $800 on Ebay.

22 - Exercise tapes

There's an market for them. Most of them have a cult following and people will pay quite a bit for them because they're so hard to find.

Nothing like going up to the counter with 5 Jane Fonda tapes right? You're going to get some weird looks when you shop the thrift correctly, I guarantee it.

What to look for:

P90x dvd sets will run you around $30 at the thrift store but you can get $150 to $200 on Ebay for them. A pumped up profit, if I do say so myself.

23 - Tom's Shoes

Hipsters also love their Toms shoes. It's a great brand and highly desired and respected in the community. Memorize the way a Tom's shoe looks. The blue tag with TOMS on the back of the heel is a great way to spot them every time.

I usually find Toms shoes at a thrift store or usually at a yard sale in a more upscale neighborhood.

Be sure to check the soles and back of the shoes as they do tend to wear out in those places.

What to look for:

The more upscale boots can be sold for $70 to $80. They can be very hard to find and people are willing to pay high prices for them.

24 - Serendipity children's books

I know you've seen this series in your local thrift store before. They are there, trust me. They usually have an interesting title along with a pony or caterpillar on the front.

People love to collect these as they are still used in classrooms today for elementary guidance counselors.

What to look for:

If you can buy these books in multiple and in hardcover then you have the possibilities for a real find. Sets of these have sold for upwards for $200 on Ebay.

25 - Hawaiian shirts

People love their Hawaiian shirts. The older the better! Look for the handmade tags and the wooden buttons. The brighter the colors and the more parrots and tikis are on the shirt then the more popular it will be to your buyers.

What to look for:

Keep your eyes open for those Paradise Found "Magnum P.I." look a like Hawaiian shirts. They can go for as high as $70 on Ebay, especially during the summer months and Halloween season.

You can still find these at your local thrift but be advised that Goodwill is starting to get smarter and is selling most vintage video games on their own online auction site.

Your best bet is to find these at yard sales around your area. Don't be afraid to ask the person running the sale if there are any other video games inside they would be wanting to sell as well. That's how you will usually find the good stuff.

What to look for:

Most anything that has Mario on it is going to be a great buy. Look for the Super Mario Allstars cartridge and if you can sell it with a tested SNES system you could easily be selling it on Ebay for $90 to $100.

27 - Disney Reader books

Parents are always looking for ways that they can share a Disney story with their kids during story time at night. It's worth taking the time to look through sold listings on Ebay so that you familiarized with the more popular ones.

What to look for:

I pick up these hardcover classics for less than a dollar at the Goodwill. You'll want to keep your eyes out for the Lilo and Stitch book as I am always able to sell that particular story for at least $30 on Amazon.

28 - Beanie Boos

The Beanie Baby craze never fully went away. It just morphed into another form. We all know what those little plushes look like but now we need to keep an eye out for the big eyed Beanie Boos. I always look these guys up just in case.

What to look for:

There are some of these beanie boos that are very valuable to collectors at this time.

For example, Treasure the unicorn is selling in the mid $200 to $300 range on Ebay as of Fall 2014. Prices do fluctuate with the seasons so always do your homework before purchasing.

29 - The Croods

This movie had great writing and it had Nicolas Cage. You can't go wrong. For some reason there were not high supplies of merchandise made for this movie so it is something I have my eye out for when I am out hunting in the thrift stores.

What to look for:

The Art of the Croods movie artwork book

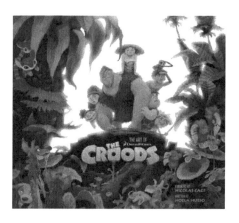

This book is highly sought after by collectors and hard to find. You can regularly get at least $100 for this book on Ebay and Amazon.

I've noticed a trend lately. Whenever there is a big ticket "comic book" movie such as X-Men or Avengers or Guardians of the Galaxy there is usually an increase in the value of certain comic books associated with the characters in the movie.

What to look for:

For example, when everyone found out that the villain in the upcoming X-Men sequel was Apocalypse the value of the comic book where the first appearance of this villain was skyrocketed.

The title of this comic is X-Factor #6. It's currently going for around $200 to $300 on Ebay. It is entirely possible that you could find a copy of this still at a flea market somewhere.

Start looking ahead to the upcoming "comic book" movies and you may be able to cash in on this trend.

31 - Scene It board games

This board game combines watching movie clips, pop culture knowledge, and hanging out with your friends.

Needless to say, it is extremely popular and some of the editions of the games are highly sought after. You will see this game new and still sealed at Goodwill all the time. It's just making sure you're picking up one that is actually worth something. Research before you buy.

What to look for:

The Star Trek Ultimate Fan Edition. This guy is huge and comes with 6 different model ships from the series as well. It will go up to $150 on Ebay. Keep you eyes open for this one!

Legos can be amazing. Once they are out of print certain lines will increase in value like you wouldn't believe.

It's not just whole sets either. The small figurines or "mini-figs" can go for large sums as well. There are whole websites dedicated solely to keeping track of what the current market value of every different lego piece out there is. Incredible.

What to look for:

If you see any oversized Lego Star Wars sets they are worth looking up every time. For example, the Super Star Destroyer set is now going for roughly $700 to $800 on Ebay which is much more than you would have originally paid for it at Walmart.

33 - Graphic novels

Graphic novels are usually a compilation of multiple comic books together or a stand alone story. Depending on the characters or story line they can be highly valuable.

What to look for:

The Life and Times of Scrooge McDuck is a graphic novel compilation which contains multiple issues of Scrooge's family history series and how he became the rich duck he is today.

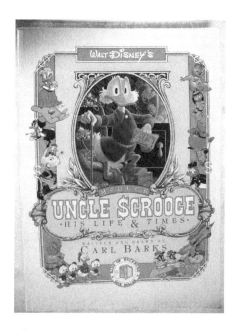

This graphic novel compilation normally goes for $150 on Ebay and is on my bucket list of things to find at a thrift store.

34 - Anime DVD sets

They may not be exactly your "cup of tea" but don't entirely discount the value of them right away.

Certain sets can be hard to find because they are out of print and also because of the subtitling on the particular set.

What to look for:

The Neon Genesis Evangelion 7 DVD set is one you may find in your local thrift store.

It currently is going on Ebay for $150 to $300. You can set the price you're wanting to get on this particular set currently as it is very hard to find.

35 - Board games

In this age of technology we can do most things using our phones and tablets. Some things just aren't the same on glass and metal though. That's why people will pay a lot of money to buy a board game they remember playing with their family and friends during their childhood.

I tend to stick mostly to board games that are still sealed. It is possible to buy opened games and resell them but you'll want to make sure that all parts are present in the set you're buying. Nobody likes an unhappy customer.

What to look for:

A highly collectible action board game is "Fireball Island". Again, make sure all the pieces are present.

This game will usually go for $300 to $400 dollars after a pretty intense bidding war.

36 - Sony Walkmen

People still love the vintage walkmen players. They can't get enough of the nostalgia and also the fact that they can listen to the radio on a workout without being tethered to their phone.

Keep an eye out for the sealed walkmen players as they can go for $100 plus on Amazon or Ebay. You can find these in your thrift store and local garage sales.

What to look for:

The Holy Grail of the walkman devices right now is the Sony TPS-L2 model which was featured prominently in the movie "Guardians of the Galaxy.

In mid 2014 this device was selling for $600 to $800 on Ebay. In Fall of 2014, this model is selling for upwards of $2,500 due to Halloween costume purchases.

Look for the bold neon colors when you're scanning the jacket section of the thrift store. The pinker the better. Also, any older sports team, college or major leagues can be great things to put on Ebay for selling.

What to look for:

Ralph Lauren Polo Sport jackets from the early 1990s are very desirable.

Keep an eye open for the bright reds and blues with the block black Ralph Lauren text. It's easy to get $100 at least for these throwback jackets.

38 - Nike Air Jordans

Sneaker heads love their shoes and they will pay out the nose to get that classic pair in their collection. One could just focus on learning all there is to know about classic and vintage basketball shoes and the payout would be worth it. If you can find these in the box still at a yard sale then even better.

What to look for:

Honestly, if you find an old pair of Jordan then take a few minutes and research them. Classic pairs will at the least go for $499 to $599 all day long on Ebay.

For example: these 1985 Carolina blue Nike Air Jordan 1s went for $650 recently.

39 - Pearl snap shirts

Everyone loves a good pearl snap shirt whether you're a rockabilly hipster or an actual cowboy. The crazier the designs around the shoulders the better. Vintage brands sell like crazy!

What to look for:

Embroidered roses and arrows are what you want to look for around the shoulders.

The "Bar C" brand screams classic 1950s and will lasso in around $100 to $150 for you on Ebay. Keep an eye out for these type of shirts at estate sales hiding out in the closets!

40 - Text Books

Timing is everything. Keep your eye out on Craigslist and college campuses around the end of the school year. You may even want to put your own posting up for buying back school books from your local college students or professors.

Text books can retain their value for years to come so don't pass up the older ones you see at thrift stores. My preferred venue for selling a text book is definitely Amazon and highly recommend that you do the same.

What to look for:

Don't judge a book by its cover. If it looks weird then it may be worth something. Case in point as follows.

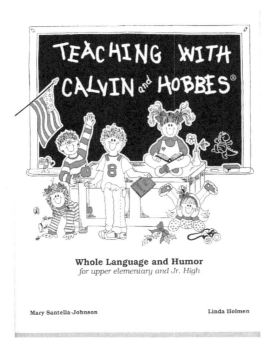

This "Calvin and Hobbes" themed teaching guide text book is extremely rare and will regularly sell on Ebay for $1,000 plus.

I remember the days of walking into a computer store and seeing the rows of those big box computer games. Those days are mostly gone now but the market is still here.

People love those old games and still want to play them. Some of them are even highly sought after by collectors as set pieces for an office.

If you can find them sealed then even better! Flea markets and antique malls are places I've had great luck in finding these hidden gems.

What to look for:

World of Warcraft Collector's Edition Box sets are highly valuable and sought after. Right now a set from 10 years ago is going for $2,000 plus on Ebay.

I could see one of these just sitting at a yard sale waiting to be found. I have also heard stories of items such as these being found in the clearance aisles of Walmart stores. The lesson is to keep your eyes open wherever you are!

You will find these hidden in the regular CD section of your thrift store or even at a yard sale. Keep your eye out for older Windows based software as it can be highly sought after. Usually it's just a jewel case and a disc but make sure you always check the disc for markings on the side where the data is kept.

What to look for:

An example for something you could look for would be "Timon and Pumbaa's Adventures in Typing".

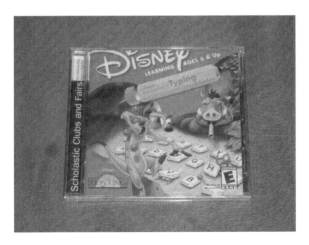

A simple CD program to the eye but I have sold this on Amazon in the past for up to $70.

The main thing to focus on is that storytelling and role playing is a part of our current culture now more than ever. People love the older original game books and want to have them as part of their collection. Don't overlook anything that looks to be part of a fantasy roleplaying game when you're at any of our sourcing locations.

What to look for:

Burn these older looking books into your retinas.

They are the original Dungeons and Dragons roleplaying books and can go up to $2,500 on Ebay.

44 - Elf Quest

Once you see the style of drawing these older graphic novels use then you won't forget it. It's unique and it's older which invokes a unique form of nostalgia akin to the Ewok movies.

I could see these working their way into a thrift store or an estate sale. The collectors are fierce for certain pieces of this brand.

What to look for:

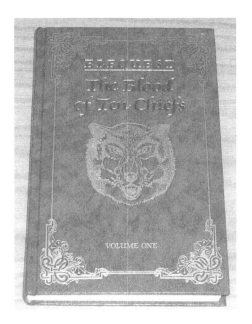

The hardback collector editions of this series can go up to $200.

Anything with Elf Quest on it is worth check out.

45 - License plates

Sometimes you can find these at a yard sale or estate sale. They're worth looking up. You can use the year of the plates to help you find the right listings on Ebay completed sales. These will sell all the time for you if you are lucky enough to have an antique booth. They are the perfect man cave decorating accessory.

What to look for:

Porcelain plates make for a huge sale on Ebay most times. Looking at completed listings for porcelain plates you will see them selling at well past $1,000.

Also, any vanity plates are worth picking up, even if they are newer plates. These plates can easily bring you up to $60 from the right buyer on Ebay.

I don't want to get started on the quality on original trilogy vs prequels but seriously there is money to be made in the original Star Wars.

This brand is so deep into all of our memories and lives that there will always be a buyer for any Star Wars item you are are trying to sell. The trick is to find the quality pieces.

What to look for:

There is some estate sale that has the original 1977 Kenner figures still in the package and is waiting for you to purchase them at $1 each. I can dream, right? Seriously, it's not out of the question.

For example, this Darth Vader original and never taken out of the package will get you up to $1,500.

47 - Transformers

I'm referring to the original 1980s ones you grew up with. I'm not talking the ones where the movies just came out in the last 10 years but the animated series or Generation 1 as you may have heard them called before. People love their original Transformer toys.

What to look for:

Generation 1 "Scorponok". A bad guy that's going to earn you a lot of good money. Having the box helps a lot for these guys.

For example, "Scorponok" has been selling recently for $500 to $600 on Ebay.

48 - He-Man

By the power of "you know what", you'd better not be passing up He-man or Skeletor when you're at the local estate sale.

His power may be in a sword and in a tiger but your power will be in the amazing profits that you can find once you research out this character line from the 1980s.

What to look for:

The He-Man figure from 1981, alone and by itself, can go up to $500 on Ebay.

I guarantee this figure is currently in at least 10 toy piles are you local town's yard sale. Knowledge is power in this game. Know your product.

49 - Back to the Future

I love Back to the Future. It's my favorite movie of all time. I am highly biased towards it and I usually end up holding onto any items I find in the local thrift store for my personal collection.

I predict 2015 will see a resurgence in collectors wanting to purchase Back to the Future themed items. I shouldn't have to explain why. If you don't know then stop reading this and watch the trilogy as part of your training for your thrift store hunts.

What to look for:

One day I will find the Krups 223 Coffina Super coffee maker at an estate sale and I will keep it for myself. If you find it you can probably get up to $200 on Ebay for it.

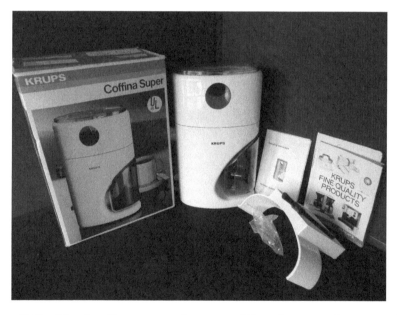

It's what "Mr. Fusion" was made out of for the movie. Watch the second movie and you'll understand.

50 - Funko collectibles

They're awesome and fun little collectible standup figures that have been made of any and every single pop culture character line in the universe.

Some of them are worth an obscene amount of money due to how rare and hard to find they are.

What to look for:

Retired figures can bring in a good amount of money on Ebay or Amazon. Social media groups can help you stay on top of what the current going price is for these figures.

For example, currently in late 2014, the "Bane" figure from "The Dark Knight Rises" movie is going for at least $100 on Ebay.

51 - Comic Con Exclusives

Every year there are big conventions held around the country that are gatherings of pop culture. Toy manufacturers will make special edition products that are only available to purchase during these weekends.

People will pay a lot of money to get their hands on these special products, trust me. It's not out of the question that one could go to these convention and have their entire trip paid for by selling a few items that were purchased at the same convention.

What to look for:

For example, a Lego Hobbit movie mini figure character, only available during that weekend, just sold on Ebay for over $2,000.

Let that sink in. $2,000. It's amazing. Your entire trip paid for itself with a little piece of plastic. Get to it.

52 - Casio calculator watches

They're fun and hipsters love them. Wear one and you'll be able to figure out that math problem at the drop of a hat. Easy money every time.

What to look for:

Look for the gold model. The DBC-611G to be exact.

If you can find this in good condition then it could get you up to $70 on Ebay easily.

53 - Seiko watches

Speaking of cool watches, here's a "terminator" of a watch. This is the watch that Arnold Schwarzenegger wears and it's a work of art.

What to look for:

Model number is H558-5009. The diving watch that Arnold wore in "Commando". It's awesome.

Someone reading this will see it in a jewelry case at a Goodwill someday. Then they'll sell it on Ebay for up to $600. Hopefully it will be you!

54 - Coleman camping gear

The Coleman name is iconic and people still love it. Whether it's a stove or a lantern or a cooler, you can be sure that there's a place for it on Ebay or your local antique booth. It's the perfect addition to any man cave.

Once you see the Coleman red or green that is usually used in their products you'll recognize it from a mile away!

What to look for:

Get to know your Coleman lanterns. They can be worth a lot of money, especially the older they are.

To the right collector an older lantern can be worth all the way up to $800 to $900.

55 - Under Armour clothing

It keeps you warm or cool in the proper season depending of course on which line of Under Armour you're wearing. Usually you will see it as a lightweight black shirt or a hoodie. I highly recommend picking them up as they are highly desirable in the athletic community.

What to look for:

Under Armour does make camouflage hunting themed apparel. If you are fortunate enough to stumble upon a coat or pants then definitely pick them up.

A coat alone can go up to $200 on Ebay depending on the season.

56 - Black Dog apparel

Only the rich and cool kids in New England have this brand. Seeing it instantly makes me think of vacation on Cape Cod.

What to look for:

Keep your eyes peeled for the grey hooded sweatshirt with the iconic "Black Dog" on the front.

These can sell on Ebay for up to $60 if you have the right buyer.

57 - Audio books

People love listening to a great book on their commute and will pay for the ability to enjoy their favorite author during their drive or bus ride.

What to look for:

If you can get an entire series of audiobooks together in a lot then there is definitely money to be made. Buy a part of the series at a thrift store or even on Ebay if the price is right.

For example, the entire audio book series of Harry Potter could get you $250 on Ebay which is a great price. The name of the game is of course getting them for a low price to begin with so that you can get the most profit.

58 - Language training courses

Business travelers are always needing quality language training courses for their international work trips. Don't be afraid to research them out at the thrift store. I've sold a Norwegian language course for $100 before. The market is out there.

What to look for:

Remember the name "Pimsleur" They make comprehensive language immersion courses.

If you can get the entire audio CD set they usually will go for up to $500. Don't let the bulkiness of it scare you from picking them up!

59 - Stand up Comedy CDs

People need to laugh and some of those old comedy CDs never got transferred to any other form of media. That being said, the only way they'll ever hear those classic bits is to buy those CDs from you.

What to look for:

Old "Bob and Tom" radio show CDs are highly desirable as the content is hard to find now.

It's not out of the question to get $30 to $40 per CD for this particular humor CD series.

60 - WWF Wrestling Teddy Bears

Super hard to find but amazingly nostalgic. It's a teddy bear dressed up as the Macho Man or Hulk Hogan. They are out there still and if you can find them still in the original plastic bag then your profits are even higher.

What to look for:

The Macho Man WWF teddy bear can sell for over $80.

These hard to find bears are super sought after by wrestling fans.

61 - Duffy teddy bears

Disney came out with a line of teddy bears that had the silhouette of Mickey Mouse's head hidden in each foot paw print. Collectors love these bears and will pay top dollar for the original bears where they are not advertised as having a "hidden Mickey" on them.

What to look for:

People spend way too much on these bears. I'm not one to judge at all because I'm more than happy to sell these bears to them.

The most sought after is a Valentine's Day themed bear from 2003.It has been selling on Ebay for $1,500.

62 - Cook books

Information is highly sought after. When that information is not available on the internet then people need to have that printed book in their hands no matter what the cost. A cook book may seem dull and boring but there are some out there that are highly collectible. Your job is to know which ones those are.

What to look for:

Julia Child is a well known cook. If you can find a first edition of "Mastering the Art of French Cooking" from 1961 then you could easily make up to $200 on Ebay.

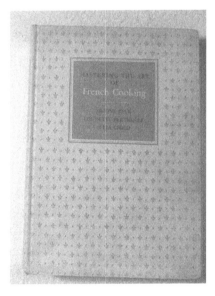

I could see this sitting on a Goodwill just waiting for someone to find it.

63 - Vintage concert shirts

Goodwill is home to a lot of hidden treasures. If you're the one to stumble upon a classic concert shirt from 20 to 30 years ago then you're about to have a good time. Persistence is the name of the game if you're going to find one of these. Hit the thrift daily and don't be afraid to go down the shirt racks one by one.

What to look for:

Old 1980s metal shirts will sell for much more than you could have imagined.

For example, this Black Sabbath shirt has recently sold on Ebay for $600. A great profit for a shirt that would have cost me $3.50 at a Goodwill.

64 - Kickstarter exclusives

This one is a longshot but if the stars align and you happen to find an item that was used as a reward for Kickstarter supporters than the profit for you will potentially be great.

What to look for:

You'd probably be finding a CD or DVD or some sort of media that was produced with the Kickstarter project.

For example,

If you had stumbled upon this pin from the Penny Arcade kickstarter in a thrift store and then put it on Ebay then you would have made $1,800 recently. Incredible.

65 - Vintage camouflage clothing

Hunters love their camo. They want to get the original design or coat they remember their grandfather wearing or whoever it was that first introduced them to hunting. You'll start to notice a trend when you are reselling vintage items. People are usually trying to buy back their memories. I love it when I get to hear the stories of why a person is buying an item.

What to look for:

One brand I look for specifically is Filson out of Seattle, Washington.

If you can find a vintage camouflage Filson coat then you are getting ready to have a good time! One just recently sold for over $400.

66 - External frame backpacks

You will find them at yard sales and estate sales usually. Look for the huge metal "n" shape on the top of the backpack. Most people will use an internal framed backpack now but there are some people that will still use the external frame ones either for decoration or even for hiking.

What to look for:

Vintage burnt orange or red. Those cool old 80s colors are going to tip you off. North Face is a good brand to keep in mind.

The older externals will usually sell on Ebay for $150 to $200.

67 - Vintage sport shirts

I'm talking about the ones from the late 1980s to early 1990s where you had the big headed caricature style sports players or the Olympic Basketball Dream Team.

What to look for:

Be sure to inspect thoroughly for holes and stains as that can effect the value of the shirt.

For example: this 1992 Dream Team Basketball shirt has been selling recently on Ebay for $60 to $80.

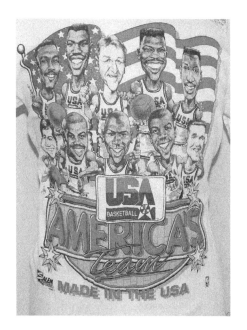

Just look at those faces!

68 - Study Bibles

A study Bible is usually seen easily by being ridiculously oversized. Keep an eye out for the ones that are made with leather as well. That will increase the value exponentially.

What to look for:

A bonded leather or calfskin leather bound Bible can get you $200 to $300 on Ebay.

69 - Mystery Science Theater 3000 DVD sets

MST3K is a highly collectible science fiction series. The main idea is you're watching a 1950s era movie that is being made fun of the entire time by a space traveler watching the movie.

What to look for:

Most of the box sets are out of print and hard to find.

For example, the Volume 9 Box set is selling regularly on Ebay for $200. You'll probably find these at a "moving away to college" yard sale.

70 - Magazine back issues

This is another time where having a photographic memory is going to serve you best when you are a thrift store picker.

What to look for:

When the information is super niche and specific that's where you can be sure the money is.

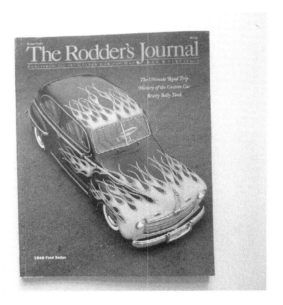

For example, this issue of The Rodder's Journal, a hotrod magazine, just sold for $46 on Ebay.

71 - American Girl dolls

My sister had one of these dolls growing up in the 1980s. Each doll was focused on a different historical period.

What to look for:

Look for dolls that are in good condition. The more accessories you can bundle with the doll then the more money you will receive for it.

For example, a "Molly" doll set was just sold on Ebay for $350.

72 - Speak 'n Spell sets

These were made popular in the 1980s. You'll want to make sure the voice chip works and that the screen is still working as well.

There is a renewed interest in these devices due to circuit benders modifying the inner workings for art projects.

What to look for:

Find and bundle all 3 of the toys in the set for maximum profits.

All 3 in the series together are fetching up to $90 on Ebay currently.

73 - Teddy Ruxpin

This guy was awesome to have when you were growing up in the 1980s. An electronic bear friend who had a tape player built into him, he would mouth along to the story as it played and blink his eyes as well. He had many different outfits, ranging from Santa Claus to hiking.

What to look for:

The key here is to have a Ruxpin where everything, including the mouth and eyes, works. Testing is essential.

If you can find one where everything is in great working condition then you could usually get up to $150 on Ebay for it.

74 - E.T. the Extra Terrestrial

Kids still love E.T., even 30 years after it was originally released. Once you start looking for him you'll be surprised at how many places you'll start to see E.T. memorabilia.

What to look for:

This one could be hard to find but look out for the E.T. Halloween mask from 1982.

Depending on the condition of the mask, you can get expect to get anywhere from $200 to $400 on Ebay.

75 - Vintage airline travel posters

I'm referring to posters from the 1950s usually depicting different travel destinations from around the world.

What to look for:

Keep an eye out for American Airlines or TWA. The poster does not have to be in 100% perfect condition as the age is the most important thing.

For example, this 1950s American Airlines New York poster just recently sold for $1,500.

76 - Metal brand signs.

As seen in the show "American Pickers", the old rusty signs with brands on them are highly collectible. The rustier the better it seems when it comes to these guys. Your best bet for finding these items is going to be at your local estate sales or auctions.

What to look for:

The more recognizable the brand, the bigger audience you'll usually have for selling.

For example, this rusty old "Texaco" sign recently sold on Ebay for close to $900.

77 - Soft drink themed products

Everyone has their favorite flavored soft drink. People love to "represent" their favorite drink by having vintage advertising or signs or even buying older bottles of the drink themselves. Your best bet for this type of thing is probably at auction houses.

What to look for:

Here's an example of buying and reselling.

Currently Amazon has Surge soda released through them only. When it's available you can get the soda for $14 for a twelve pack from Amazon. People are then selling those twelve packs on Ebay for $100 each. Just another example of how a person can resell any product if there is a market available for it.

78 - Talkboy

In the movie "Home Alone 2" there was an amazing device introduced called the Talkboy. It was a personal hand held cassette tape recorder and it was a glorious one at that.

What to look for:

Put this image into your memory banks.

If you find just the Talkboy itself it usually goes on Ebay for $30. If you are lucky enough to find it never opened then you can get upwards of $100 plus on Ebay.

79 - Charlie Brown themed items

Charlie Brown has been a part of our culture for at least 50 years now. Everyone knows Charlie Brown and his dog, Snoopy. The Christmas special is played over and over every year. There's even a new movie being released soon with the characters.

What to look for:

In 2009 there were Peanuts gang themed action figures that were released which are now extremely rare.

For example, the Peppermint Patty figure has sold recently for over $150 on Ebay. Keep an eye out for these at places like garage sales and thrift stores.

80 - Patagonia

Patagonia is a high end camping and outdoors themed brand. It can be found on everything from backpacks and fanny packs to shirts and coats. Commit the logo to your memory as it can easily turn into potentially huge profits for yourself.

What to look for:

Look for the puffer coats when you're in the clothing section of the thrift store or when you're looking at yard sales in the more

upscale part of town.

You can expect these puffer coats to go up to $150 on Ebay.

81 - Vintage typewriters

Keep your eyes peeled for the vintage and older typewriters. You can usually pick them up for a few dollars at your local small town auction. There has been a real resurgence in the popularity of these items due to current decorating trends and indie arts and crafts.

What to look for:

Make sure all the keys are still on the typewriter before you purchase. Be aware that sometimes the keys themselves are worth more by themselves than if you sold the typewriter as a complete object. Make sure to fully research out both of these options before you post the item for sale on your preferred marketplace.

For example:

A lot of all the keys off of a Remington typewriter can bring up to $60 to $70 on Ebay while sometimes the whole typewriter can bring anywhere from $39 to over $100 on the same marketplace. It is crucial that you put your work in researching to make sure you make the most profit with your purchase.

82 - Lunchboxes

Lunchboxes are a piece of Americana that most buyers can still associate with. They can be plastic or metal depending on the era that it is from. Characters are usually found on the outside of the main lunchbox itself but keep your eyes open for the thermos as well to complete the set.

What to look for:

Any cartoon or rock band is worth doing a quick search on Ebay

completed and sold listings for.

For example: if you can find this original Beatles lunchbox from the mid 1960s era you could easily be making $1,000 to $1,500 on Ebay. I could see this being found at an estate sale although the asking price could be higher than what you might usually pay at the thrift.

83 - Kitchen utility replacement parts

You may not have huge sales but it is a good thing to keep in mind for quick flips of items on Ebay.

Every person out there has a device in their kitchen that has a breakable part that will or has broken on them. That part is usually hard to find or expensive to purchase by itself. I know plenty of people that will buy broken kitchen devices just to get certain parts out of them for reselling on Ebay. Search for completed and sold listings for "replacement parts" on Ebay to familiarize yourself with the most sought after parts that you could then be finding at your local thrift store or auction for much cheaper than retail.

What to look for:

Blender replacement parts are highly sought after. Remember the name "Vitamix" as they are top of the food chain currently when it comes to blenders.

For example: this Vitamix 2 Part Lid Top Plug is currently selling for $60 on Ebay.

84 - Jewelry

This is a subject I need to become more familiarized with. I have never looked into the jewelry lock case at my local thrift except only to check for GameBoy games which sometimes are put in there.

Any easy way to be able to test to see if a piece is gold or not is to use a small handheld magnet over the piece of jewelry. If the piece is attracted to the magnet then it usually means that the piece is fake. If the piece is not attracted to the magnet than it may be worth looking closer into the piece as gold is not attracted to magnets.

What to look for:

Anything unique and vintage with a gold appearance to it. You might have more luck with flea markets or out of the way thrift stores to find actual jewelry gems like these.

For example: this rose gold wedding band from 1863 sold on Ebay recently for just over $100. Keep your eyes open. The treasures are out there.

85 - Cameras

It's worth at least having a basic knowledge of cameras and cameras lenses. Brands you'll want to be aware of are Canon, Zeiss, and Nikon. If it looks big and expensive then you need to look up the model number and then chances are that it's probably expensive. You can sometimes pick up classic lenses at yard sales for $10 to $20 that are worth way more than that on Ebay.

Always be sure to look for cracks or imperfections in the camera lens. This can highly downgrade the value or cause a return you will not want to deal with.

What to look for:

For example, this Nikon 70-300 lens just recently sold on Ebay for $250.

Remember, if it looks awesome then look it up because it probably is. Go with your gut but also check with Ebay completed sold listings.

86 - "Mad Men" themed items

I'm talking of course about the all encompassing genre of vintage "cool dudes in suits and looking snazzy" type of antique decorating items. If you're at an estate sale and your "picker sense" is going wild over an item then buy it if you can for a low price. There is risk involved so take the time before hand to research what's currently hot and what to look for. Knowledge is power in this game every single time.

What to look for:

I'm not a smoker but art deco style smoking accessories from the 1960s time period is exactly what you are looking for.

For example:

This roulette wheel style cigarette holder featured on the main character's desk in the show is currently fetching up to $150 on Ebay.

87 - Old Photos

If you're at an estate sale and there is a pile of old black and white style photos for a low cost then I would highly recommend to pick them up. They are definitely best sold on a marketplace such as Ebay. Research is key here as you will find there are certain themes in older photographs that will make you a lot of money.

What to look for:

Specifics. specifics. specifics.

For example: this older photograph just sold recently on Ebay for

a substantial amount.

The subject matter is the Chinese Labour Corp Group at Boulogne, France in 1918. Very specific and a lot of great keywords to drive traffic to the auction as well. It was originally listed for $20 and ended up selling for approximately $850. Amazing.

88 - Old Postcards

The same applies to these as it does to the page on older photos you just read. However, a word of caution here, don't become a hoarder of older photos and postcards. Be selective in the items that you are buying. Unless of course you want to have your spare bedroom wallpapered with the ones that haven't sold for months and in that case then good luck to you.

What to look for:

The older and more vintage the subject matter is the better. Also the more specific detailed keywords you can use in your listing the more eyes are going to be focused on your auction as well.

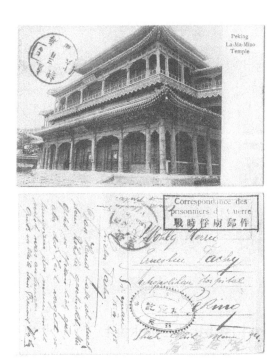

For example:

This postcard from 1918 of the La Ma Miao Temple in Peking, China ended up selling for almost $400 and was listed for less than $20. Amazing profit margins!

89 - Harley Davidson themed items

Learn to recognize the Harley Davidson logo on shirts, stuffed animals, and many other things. Motorcycle riders love the Harley Davidson brand and are constantly looking on Ebay for new items to add to their collection. Keep an eye out at yard sales and thrift stores for Harley Davidson items you can add to your online store.

What to look for:

If you can find a higher end leather riding jacket with the words "Harley Davidson", a screaming eagle logo, or something similar

then you may have just hit the jackpot.

Jackets in this line can go for as high as $500 to $600 on Ebay and you will have many people watching and bidding on your item. Everyone loves a Harley!

90 - Cast Iron Skillets

Most people will remember the classic cast iron pan from their camping excursions when they were growing up. People still love to use a frying pan when they are cooking out. It's the flavor that it gives their food and the way it cooks it that you just can't replicate any other way.

What to look for:

Look for the name "Griswold". It is the Cadillac of antique cast iron skillets.

For example:

A rare #13 Griswold cast iron skillet just sold on Ebay for over $700. It has 13 different bidders on it over the duration of the auction. Griswold is highly sought after and should be added to your picker memory banks.

91 - Vintage vacuum refill bags

This may have caught you by surprise but some people have the older vacuums in use in their house. The thing is that you can't just walk into a Walmart and buy a replacement bag for these older vacuums.

You will start to see these at thrift stores everywhere. They're out there and people will pay good money to still be able to use their old trusty vacuums. You can set the cost when it comes to these.

What to look for:

The older looking the bags are the more they're usually worth. Amazon is a great place to sell these on because most people will end up looking for them there. Ebay is your next best

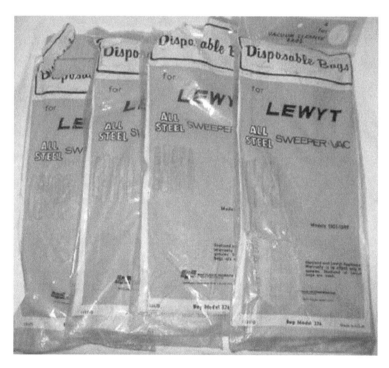

marketplace to end up selling them.

You can usually get around $35 for these on Amazon.

92 - Satin jackets

These jackets are one of the most lucrative items you can look for. Usually you can pick them up for $5 to $10 at the thrift store and you should be able to get $75 to $100 for them depending on the subject material.

What to look for:

I look for the button up vintage college sports team related jackets as those for me have been the most lucrative.

For example: this University of California Starter jacket recently sold on Ebay for $400.

93 - Bronze material items

Bronze is a great metal to use as a decorating accent. It makes anything look sophisticated and refined. It is the perfect metal for use in a library decorating item.

I look for bronze statues for purchase at auctions and estates sales but it isn't out of the question to find them at thrift stores. Your best marketplace for reselling these items would be on Ebay or an antique booth.

What to look for:

Look for eagles, lions, and various other animals.

For example: this bronze eagle status sold recently on Ebay for $550.

94 - "How to play" instrument books

You may see books at Goodwills such as how to play all the songs from a certain artist's cd on a guitar or a piano.

The older the songbook then the more rare it could possibly be, which of course will net you more profits.

Keep an eye out for Beatles themed music books and anything that seems to be unique such as banjos or harps.

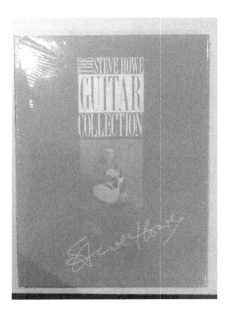

What to look for:

Here's an example. This sealed guitar book from 1993 sold recently for over $300. It's definitely important to do your research in this category.

95 - Snapback hats.

It's a quick way to make a loud fashion statement and also show everyone around you who your sports team loyalties are.

These hats are definitely very popular at this time and Ebay and Etsy are your best marketplace to sell them.

Make sure the rim is not bent and that there is no sweat on the inside brim. If you still have the tags on the hat then even better.

What to look for:

This University of Washington Huskies trucker snapback just recently sold for $150. Use your imagination when sourcing these hats!

96 - Vintage patches

I'm talking about iron on patches or sew on patches here. They come in many shapes and sizes and people love them. You can put an old name tag patch on a bowling shirt and make it instantly awesome. You can put an older hiking patch on a backpack and transform it into a cool old hiking bag.

What to look for:

Original military patches from the various wars can be huge on Ebay. Keep an eye out for these at estate sales.

For example: this Super Jolly Green Giant helicopter military patch recently went for over $800 on Ebay with a large amount of bidders. Patches are serious items.

97 - Magic cards

There are many different types of collectible card games and Magic is one of them. Some of these cards are worth a large amount of money. You could spend hours and hours researching the current value of these cards but I've found it's worth it to have a friend who is an expert in the category (#woofwoof).

What to look for:

Keep an eye out for the extremely rare Black Lotus card. There are not many left out there in the wild. But if you find one you'll be able to go on vacation for a fair amount of time. These cards have sold recently on Ebay for anywhere from $8,000 to $20,000.

98 - Cassette tapes

You may think that this a dead way to enjoy music but it is worth taking a minute to look over the cassette section at your local thrift store. You'll be surprised what you'll find there. Everything from old stand up comedy to classic rock albums will be there.

What to look for:

Original demo tapes of bands can be a goldmine.

For example: this autographed demo tape duo from the band Tegan and Sara just sold on Ebay for over $1,770.

99 - Blank recordable media

Keep an eye out for older recordable VHS tape multipacks or recordable audio cassette tapes as well. There is still quite a market for these tapes in places such as recording studios or the Soviet Union. I'm serious. Always be thinking outside the box!

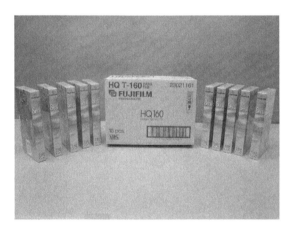

What to look out out for:

Look for sealed multipacks of VHS tapes for cheap at the thrift store or at estate sales. You can usually sell these on Amazon or Ebay for an easy $35 or higher like the ones pictured.

100 - Transcriber machines

Keep an eye out for micro cassette transcriber machines used by court recorders. I have found these at Goodwill outlets before and they still sell pretty well.

What to look for:

If you are fortunate enough to find one in the box still then you can easily get as high as $500 on Ebay as someone recently did for this model pictured.

101 - 1980s Boomboxes

I'm talking about those big lift it over your shoulder and perch it there cassette playing monstrosities that you remember from the older rap videos.

People want those and if you can find one in a thrift store or a garage sale then you are going to make some money!

What to look for:

Look for anything that looks like what you see in the picture above. If it's in the box then leave it in the box! These can go anywhere from $600 to almost $2,000 on Ebay! Amazing.

Conclusion

You now have an arsenal of information at your fingertips. Keep your smart phone with you and use this guide as a reference when you're out searching for that "buried treasure"

I recommend to keep this book downloaded on your Kindle app on your smart phone so you can easily use this as reference guide in your next thrift store visit.

Visit **www.facebook.com/thethriftprofessor**. It's a place where I primarily share about my latest thrift finds daily and where you can be part of the community!

Finally, if you enjoyed this book, then I'd like to ask you for a favor, would you be kind enough to leave a review for this book on Amazon? It'd be greatly appreciated!

Thank you and good luck!

Check Out My Other Books

Below you'll find some of my other popular books that are popular on Amazon and Kindle as well. Simply click on the links below to check them out. Alternatively, you can visit my author page on Amazon to see other work done by me.

"How to turn Garbage into Gold: 101 Kid's Books you can find at Thrift Stores and Garage Sales to sell on Ebay and Amazon"

"How to turn Garbage into Gold: 101 Plush Toys you can find at Thrift Stores and Garage Sales to sell on Ebay and Amazon"

"Tiny House Living: 101 Ways to Save Money and Pay off Debt by Living a Minimalist Lifestyle"

"Blinks the Hamster Gets off the Debt Wheel: A Story of How You can get rid of your Student Loans and your Credit Card Debt."

-If the links do not work, for whatever reason, you can simply search for these titles on the Amazon website to find them.

CPSIA information can be obtained at www.ICGtesting.com
Printed in the USA
LVOW01s0259040615

441049LV00035B/3341/P